HAL•LEONARD
Classical
PLAY-ALONG™

Volume 7

Johann Sebastian
BACH
(1685-1750)

Violin Concerto in A Minor, Op. 1,

T0101508

ISBN 978-1-4234-6244-6

HAL•LEONARD®
CORPORATION
7777 W. BLUEMOUND RD. P.O. BOX 13819 MILWAUKEE, WI 53213

In Australia Contact:
Hal Leonard Australia Pty. Ltd.
4 Lentara Court
Cheltenham, Victoria, 3192 Australia
Email: ausadmin@halleonard.com.au

Visit Hal Leonard Online at
www.halleonard.com

Preface

The Hal Leonard Classical Play-Along™ series allows you to work through great classical works systematically and at any tempo with accompaniment.

Tracks 2-4 on the CD demonstrate the concert version of each movement. After tuning your instrument to Track 1 you can begin practicing the piece. Using the Amazing Slow-Downer technology included on the CD, you can adjust the recording to any tempo you like without altering the pitch. (Note that when using Amazing Slow-Downer, the CD will stop after each track instead of playing continuously.) The full cadenzas are played only in the concert version.

- Track No. ⬜1 – tuning notes
- Track numbers in circles ◯ – concert version
- Track numbers in diamonds ◆ – play-along version

CONCERT VERSION

Alexey Bruni, Violin

Russian Philharmonic Orchestra Moscow

Konstantin Krimets, Conductor

CONCERTO

for Violin in A minor, BWV 1041

I ②

J. S. Bach (1685 - 1750)
Edited by H. Scherz

Allegro moderato

3

4

116

121

127

132

137

141

148

154

161

166

11 **Allegro assai**